Epilepsy Book

For kids

by Layla Reid

First published in 2012 by Pomegranate Books

© Mark and Sarah Reid 2012

ISBN 978-1-84289-019-6

Printed and bound in the UK

Pomegranate Books, Bristol
www.pomegranatebooks.co.uk

The publishers would like to
thank the following organisations:

Epilepsy Action
Epilepsy Society
Young Epilepsy

for their advice and support
in the creation of this book.

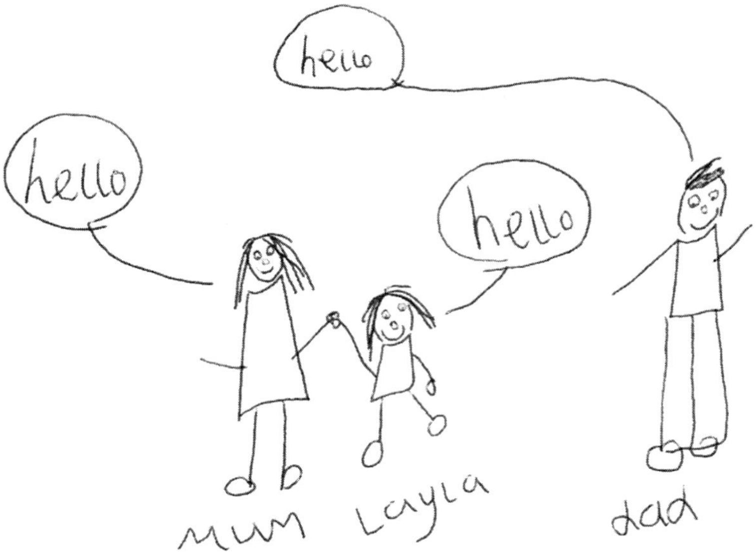
hello
hello
hello
mum
Layla
dad

Hello, my name is Layla and my mummy has epilepsy. Maybe your mummy, daddy or someone else in your family has epilepsy. I hope this book will let you know what to do if they have a seizure.

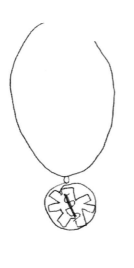

My mums
special
necklace

My Mummy wears a special necklace to tell people she has epilepsy. I show this to adults who help her when she has a seizure.

Sometimes my mummy has seizures where she gets very confused and struggles to speak. I know she needs help. I help mummy to sit down and call daddy to come and help. I keep calm and reassure mum "it's ok mummy."

Sometimes my Mummy has seizures where she falls to the ground and shakes. I call for an adult. Then I reassure Mummy and put something soft under her head. When the seizure has finished the adult will put Mummy on her side in the recovery position.

When my mummy
has a seizure
I try to move
things out of the way
that might hurt her.
I never put anything
in her mouth and I
never give her a
drink or food.

IF I cant Find an adult, I know how to call 999 for an ambulance. My Mummy put a list of phone numbers by the phone so I can call for our family or an ambulance for help.

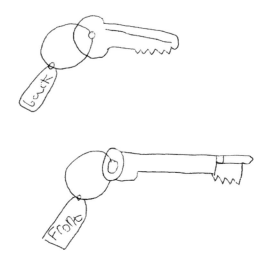

My mummy has written Front door and Back door on her keys so I can let the ambulance people in to look after Mummy.

Mummy only cooks
when daddy is home
because she might
have a seizure and
we dont want to have
a Fire.

When Mummy baths me
daddy is always home
in case she has a
Seizure.

When mummy has a shower she <u>always</u> takes the bath plug out in case she has a seizure. She doesn't take baths only showers. She only has a shower when daddy is at home.

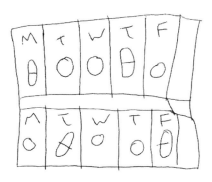

Every morning and night MuMMy must always take her tablets - but I must never touch them or I would be very poorly.

Bus Pass
Sarah
reid

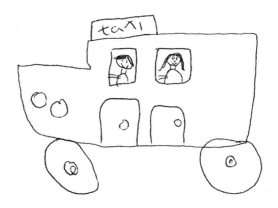

taxi

Mummy does not
drive at the moment
But she has a special
bus Pass and a
taxi takes her
to work.

When my brother or sister comes I will teach them how to look after Mummy too.

Further information on
many aspects of epilepsy
can be found at the following websites:

Epilepsy Action
www.epilepsy.org.uk

Epilepsy Society
www.epilepsysociety.org.uk

Young Epilepsy
www.youngepilepsy.org.uk